curious about

DOGS

BY M. K. OSBORNE

AMICUS • AMICUS INK

What are you

curious about?

CHAPTER THREE

Dog Behavior and Training

PAGE

14

Curious About is published
by Amicus and Amicus Ink
P.O. Box 227
Mankato, MN 56002
www.amicuspublishing.us

Copyright © 2021 Amicus.
International copyright reserved in all countries.
No part of this book may be reproduced in any
form without written permission from the publisher.

Editor: Alissa Thielges
Designer: Kathleen Petelinsek
Photo researcher: Bridget Prehn

Library of Congress Cataloging-in-Publication Data
Names: Osborne, M. K., author.
Title: Curious about dogs / by M. K. Osborne.
Description: Mankato, MN : Amicus, [2021] | Series:
Curious about pets | Includes bibliographical references and
index. | Audience: Ages 6–9 | Audience: Grades 2–3
Identifiers: LCCN 2019053806 (print) | LCCN 2019053807
(ebook) | ISBN 9781681519661 (library binding) | ISBN
9781681526133 (paperback) | ISBN 9781645490517 (pdf)
Subjects: LCSH: Dogs—Juvenile literature.
Classification: LCC SF426.5 .K59 2021 (print) |
LCC SF426.5 (ebook) | DDC 636.7—dc23
LC record available at https://lccn.loc.gov/2019053806
LC ebook record available at https://lccn.loc.gov/2019053807

Photos © Shutterstock/Dorottya Mathe cover, 1, Eric Isselee
2, 5, 6, 21 (German shepherd), Alexey Androsov 2 (left), 11
(top), Jackie Neff 3, 16–17, PNPImages 5 (snow background),
WilleeCole Photography 6–7, Goldmoon 8, Mindscape
Studio 9, Double Brain 11 (bottom), alexei_tm 12, Kkolosov
13, Enna8982 15, Ching Louis Liu 18–19, bigandt.com 20,
Africa Studio (Labrador) 21, Irina Oxilixo Danilova (golden
retriever) 21, mala_koza (bulldog) 21, Jagodka (poodle) 21

DOG COMMUNICATION

Why do dogs bark?

Simply put, dogs bark to get your **attention**. It is one way they tell us how they feel. Maybe your dog wants to play or go for a walk. Maybe someone is at the door. A bark can also mean "hello" or "I don't like that!" A calm dog usually doesn't bark.

One way a dog communicates is by barking.

Why do dogs sniff each other's butts?

DID YOU KNOW?
When dogs meet, they prefer to sniff each other's butts. It is less threatening than meeting nose to nose.

Dogs' butts have special **glands** that have a smell. They tell information about the dog. Is it a girl or boy? Is it looking for a **mate**? Dogs sniff each other to find out. They have really good noses. Dogs can smell 100 million times better than you.

A butt sniff for dogs is like a handshake for people.

Why does my dog howl?

Ah-woo! You've probably heard the sound. This means a dog is lonely. Like wolves, dogs are **pack** animals. They like to be around people and other animals. When no one is around, they howl to find their pack members. Some dogs howl at sirens. The sirens sound like other dogs howling.

The sound of a
howl can travel
for miles.

CHAPTER TWO

Why does my dog wag its tail?

Wagging fans a dog's butt glands. This helps spread their scent. A lot of wagging could mean excitement. That dog really wants to meet you. The slower the wag, the more unsure a dog is. A tucked tail hides the dog's scent. This dog does not want to be noticed. It could be scared.

This dog is alert.

Suspicious

DID YOU KNOW?
A dog wagging its tail to the right is relaxed. Wagging to the left means a dog is upset.

Playful

Fearful

This dog is upset.

Why does my dog bend down with her butt in the air?

Is her tail wagging? She wants to play! This is called a "play bow." Grab her favorite toy and give it a toss. Or run around with her.

If a dog growls or shows its teeth, do not try to play. She is not friendly. She might be upset. Leave her alone. She needs time to calm down.

This dog wants
to play.

How do dogs learn tricks?

Dogs learn best through rewards. They are very **motivated** by treats. Try this: hold a treat in a closed fist. When your dog paws at your hand, open it. Do this again. Now when she paws your hand, say, "Shake." Your dog will learn that shaking gets her a tasty reward.

DID YOU KNOW?
Your dog understands about the same number of words and gestures as a two-year-old child.

Shaking hands is
an easy trick to
teach your dog.

How do I keep my dog from chewing my stuff?

This dog may have been bored.

Dogs like to explore with their mouths. Puppies do this more than older dogs. But even adult dogs can get bored. That's when they might chew on your stuff. To prevent this, keep your stuff out of reach. Give your dog toys he can chew on. You can play with him so he isn't bored.

DID YOU KNOW?
Like humans, puppies have baby teeth that fall out. It can hurt when the adult teeth grow in. Chew toys help.

Why do dogs pee in 10 different spots on a walk?

Sniff. Squat. Pee. It's like doggie social media. Dogs pee to leave messages to other dogs. What are they like? How do they feel? What **gender** are they? A lot can be found out from their pee. When your pup smells another dog's pee, he may leave his own "message." Now the other dog can learn about him.

This dog wants to tell other dogs that he was here.

Why do some dogs eat weird things, like grass, rocks, or even poop?

Puppies put everything in their mouths.

They may just like the taste. Yes, even poop! *Eww.*
Some dogs learn this from other dogs. Mama dogs
eat their puppies' poop. Then **predators** can't find
the pups. Sick dogs sometimes eat plants or dirt.
It makes them throw up. Rocks are not safe to eat.
They can't be digested. A dog may need surgery
to remove them.

LABRADOR RETRIEVER

GERMAN SHEPHERD

GOLDEN RETRIEVER

FRENCH BULLDOG

POODLE

ASK MORE QUESTIONS

I want a pet dog. What breed would be best for me?

What other tricks can I teach my dog?

Try a BIG QUESTION: How can dogs help people?

SEARCH FOR ANSWERS

Search the library catalog or the Internet.
A librarian, teacher, or parent can help you.

Using Keywords
Find the looking glass.

Keywords are the most important words in your question.

?

If you want to know about:

- kinds of dogs, type: DOG BREEDS

- how to teach your dog tricks, type: TEACH MY DOG TRICKS

- how dogs help people, type: DOGS HELPING PEOPLE

FIND GOOD SOURCES

Here are some good, safe sources you can use in your research. Your librarian can help you find more.

Books

Listening to Your Dog by Michael J. Rosen, 2019.

A Kid's Guide to Dogs by Arden Moore, 2020.

Internet Sites

AKC: Dog Breed Selector
https://www.akc.org/dog-breed-selector
The AKC is the American Kennel Club. This group is a good source of information about dogs.

27 Dog Tricks You Can Teach Your Dog Right Now
https://www.loveyourdog.com/tricks/
At Love Your Dog.com, experienced dog owners share tips and videos for teaching your dog tricks and caring for your dog.

Every effort has been made to ensure that these websites are appropriate for children. However, because of the nature of the Internet, it is impossible to guarantee that these sites will remain active indefinitely or that their contents will not be altered.

SHARE AND TAKE ACTION

Volunteer at an animal shelter.

Offer to pet sit for a neighbor.

Be safe around dogs.
Learn their body language and know when it is okay to pet or play with a dog.

With an adult, take your dog to a dog park.
Watch them interact with other dogs.

GLOSSARY

attention A person's interest and actions towards something.

gender The sex of a person or creature.

gland An organ in the body that makes chemicals and releases a substance or smell.

mate The male or female partner of a pair of animals.

motivate To interest someone in doing something.

pack A group of animals, like dogs or wolves, that live together.

predator An animal that hunts other animals for food.

INDEX

About the Author

M. K. Osborne is a children's writer and editor who lives in Minnesota. As an animal lover, Osborne enjoyed researching and writing about pet behavior and communication and hopes to inspire kids to pursue their own inquiries about pets.